SELF-GUIDED EMDR THERAPY
HEALING FROM ANXIETY, ANGER, STRESS, DEPRESSION, PTSD & EMOTIONAL TRAUMA

SELF-GUIDED EMDR THERAPY
HEALING FROM ANXIETY, ANGER, STRESS, DEPRESSION, PTSD & EMOTIONAL TRAUMA

Katherine Andler

Cover Image: Intographics

CONTENTS

INTRODUCTION

When I *wrote Self-Administered EMDR Therapy: Freedom from Anxiety, Anger and Depression* in 2013 it was as though I'd broken the magician's code. I'd exposed the eight-step procedure that was the cornerstone of EMDR therapy. And I wasn't a therapist.

Criticism came largely from EMDR therapists who repeated a dictum that is part of the EMDR training; that the therapy must always be done by a trained practitioner. Clients risk destabilization, and he who is his own therapist has a fool for a client, they said. Destabilization can occur, but usually in clients with severe symptoms, undiagnosed dissociative disorders, and when those clients seek help from therapists who don't prepare them enough with grounding techniques. Those with severe PTSD or other emotional issues should obviously seek professional help, but even therapists have a dilemma when a client is presenting with signs of destabilization. Carrying their trauma is making the client feel unstable, but the therapy that heals the trauma may also destabilize them. The old adage that it will get worse before it will get better is never more appropriate.

When *Self-Administered EMDR Therapy* was published, most readers were glad to have the mysterious EMDR procedure finally laid out. They could now make an informed choice about whether to do it at home or with a therapist, or if EMDR was even the right treatment for them.

For those of us with mild to moderate symptoms, though we may find daily life unpleasant and frustrating at times, we can function. We aren't constantly living on an unbearable precipice. And we are capable of deciding whether we can handle the contents of our own minds or need to seek professional support.

As one of my readers stated, it is condescending to suggest this cannot be done on your own. I have used this psychotherapy hundreds of times by myself to heal trauma, including target events that I'd rated 9's and 10's on the scale of disturbance. Thankfully, there weren't too many of those!

Self-guided EMDR was just one sword in my armor on a journey to heal the Complex PTSD caused by childhood and secondary trauma. I also used Emotional Freedom Technique (EFT), self-enquiry, and meditation. My biggest breakthroughs usually came from EMDR, however.

If you choose to try EMDR at home, I always suggest practicing first using an innocuous target event (mine was a paper cut), before moving on to the bigger stuff. Be prepared also for some small traumas to be a lot bigger than you first thought.

One of the things I love about EMDR is that it puts you, the client, in control, (something we may not have had very much of when our traumas were taking place.) This book gives you back even more control by giving you all the information, so you know exactly what to expect. The workbook and journal is a good way to prepare for EMDR therapy at home or with a practitioner.

I wish you strength and healing on your journey.
Katherine Andler

A BRIEF HISTORY OF EMDR

Eye Movement Desensitization and & Reprocessing (EMDR) therapy was founded and developed by Dr Francine Shapiro.

In 1987, Shapiro was a PhD student at the Professional School of Psychological Studies in San Diego. According to her account, she was out walking in a park when she noticed that the emotional impact of the negative thoughts she was experiencing decreased when she moved her eyes side to side. As she began working through other disturbing thoughts, deliberately moving her eyes, she noticed the same diminishing effect on her symptoms.

Her initial research led her to putting forward Eye Movement Desensitization (EMD) as a treatment for PTSD and other trauma issues. After conducting further studies, Shapiro developed the therapy and added 'reprocessing' to the procedure to create Eye Movement Desensitizing and Reprocessing therapy, or EMDR for short.

This however wasn't the first time eye movements had been used as part of a therapeutic treatment. Eye Movement Pattern Interruption Therapy (now Eye Movement Integration or EMI) was introduced in 1981 by Robert Dilts, and was based on both Dilts's own 1977 research into mind processing and eye movements, and Milton H. Erickson's work in interrupting long-term behavioral patterns. Unlike EMDR, which uses fast, horizontal eye movements, EMI uses slow eye movements and a variety of different eye locations. These eye positions are based on Neuro-Linguistic Programming methods. EMI therapy is used in the treatment of PTSD, phobias and any other issues that require quick intervention and does not require the patient to experience regression.

While some have questioned the serendipitous nature of Shapiro's discovery, Bruce Grimley went further in 2014, by suggesting that the use of eye movement to heal trauma was in fact an idea that came from Dr John Grinder (the co-creator of NLP). It should be noted though that the eye movements used in NLP are quite different, although they are eye movements nonetheless.

The much larger question of whether EMDR is truly effective pivots around whether the eye movements have any effect. Some experts have claimed that without the bilateral stimulation, EMDR is no different to exposure therapy, which has been used to successfully treat PTSD, phobias and anxiety disorders. What most experts seem to agree on is that no one, not even Shapiro, seem to be able to explain how EMDR works to resolve trauma.

WHAT IS EMDR?

EMDR uses bilateral stimulation, or side-to-side eye movements, to reprocess disturbing memories. Research has indicated that the bilateral eye movements performed in EMDR may replicate the rapid eye movements (REM) during the dream stage of sleep. Scientists have long believed that during REM sleep our brains process the events of the day, including our emotions, beliefs and physical sensations. If the brain does not process these properly, memories may become lodged and can cause us problems further down the line. Sometimes the symptoms of trauma don't appear for months, years, and even decades afterwards.

Some therapists use bilateral tapping (often on the top of the client's hands) in addition to the eye stimulation. Tapping has its roots in EFT (Emotional Freedom Technique.) Dual attention stimulation (bilateral eye movements and tapping) unlocks the unprocessed memory, releases the painful emotions and sensations, and allows the brain to let go of the beliefs that hold us back. Anxiety, anger, and depression are just a few of the symptoms of having unprocessed, maladaptive memories stuck in our brains.

After EMDR therapy, your memories may seem faded. Some bits of information, deemed unimportant to our survival and future well being, may be completely discarded. However, EMDR does not delete memories. After all, removing a memory in its entirety from our life history will prevent us from learning its lesson. Painful experiences (once processed properly) make us stronger and wiser, and prevent us from having to go through the same experiences again. EMDR simply changes the way painful memories are stored, so that when we think about them they no longer trigger negative emotions or sensations. What is more, with the installation of a positive cognition to replace the negative belief, you may even feel grateful for the experience.

WHAT CAN EMDR BE USED FOR?

Initially, EMDR was used to treat major traumas, including Post Traumatic Stress Disorder (PTSD) experienced by war veterans and survivors of sexual assault. Though this therapy is relatively new, research is continuously discovering its effects on a wider range of emotional issues.

While most people think of trauma as being caused by major events, such as going to war, sexual abuse, or sustaining a serious injury, trauma can also be caused by much 'smaller' everyday incidents which haven't been processed. Francine Shapiro notes that the smaller events can actually cause much more severe symptoms of distress than major traumas. Something as 'minor' as being called "stupid" could be enough to trigger trauma symptoms. Therefore, any disturbing memory that causes an emotional and physiological reaction is a good target for EMDR therapy.

Although EMDR has not been proved to have an effect on panic disorders or phobias, some therapists argue that EMDR can be successfully used on any event that the client finds disturbing.

Examples of Issues that EMDR can treat

Anxiety and panic
Depression
Anger
Dysfunctional attachment
Embarrassment
Post-traumatic stress disorder (PTSD)
Sleep problems, including nightmares and disrupted sleep
Performance anxiety
Driving issues
Unresolved grief
Eating disorders
Chronic pain
Phobias
Addictions
Childhood experiences, including bullying, insensitive adults, parental discord, death, and divorce
Major traumas such as serious injuries or life threatening situations

War trauma

Abuse and assaults (sexual, physical, emotional)

Emotionally charged experiences, including family arguments

Work problems

Stress

Poor relationship choices

Over-reacting to normal situations

WHY SOME MEMORIES BECOME 'STUCK'

All of us experience distressing and disturbing events in our lives from time to time. In normal circumstances the brain processes these events during sleep by making new connections, discarding the bits of information that are unimportant, and transforming negative thoughts and sensations into lessons learned. It is a process that enables us to adapt and survive. However, sometimes an event may occur that is so disturbing that it overloads the brain and prevents it from completing this all-important memory-processing task. Instead, the memory gets stored along with the physical sensations and negative emotions, where it is easily, and often repeatedly, triggered in our everyday lives.

Unprocessed memories can impact on seemingly unrelated areas of our lives, which are triggered by things or people that remind us of the event. Although the cause may not always be obvious, the negative emotional symptoms (such as anger, anxiety, depression, fear etc) are easier to identify. So, the woman who looks a lot like that teacher who humiliated you as a child may trigger flashbacks of fear and embarrassment. The sound of a car backfiring may trigger the panic you felt when you heard a gunshot. The smell of a certain aftershave may trigger images of a passed loved one and unresolved grief.

Let us look at the first example of the teacher in a little more depth. Imagine that when you were ten years old an angry teacher called you stupid in front of your class because you got a math question wrong. Your body was suddenly flooded with adrenaline and you felt panic. The entire class turned to look at you, which added to your distress. You wanted to challenge the teacher's assumption but didn't because you were afraid of angering her more.

If your brain does its processing uninterrupted, it might conclude several positive things about this event:

That the teacher was most likely having a bad day or she is generally bad tempered. In either case you would conclude that it wasn't personal and you weren't to blame for her angry outburst. Furthermore, you might question why somcone would lose their temper so easily. Perhaps something triggered an old memory of her own?)

That you are smart and intelligent; your grades prove this, even if math isn't your forte

That it is OK to make a mistake

That you don't have to be good at every subject

That the majority of the other kids in the class looking at you probably weren't on the teacher's side

That if anyone calls you stupid in the future you will calmly disagree, or perhaps have a quiet word with them later

That you now know the correct answer to the math problem and it may be useful if you have to do a test

That you have been attending school for years and this is the first time you've been humiliated by a teacher, so it is unlikely to happen again.

There are, of course, many other positive conclusions and adaptations that could be made from this incident depending on what the brain already knows. However, if something disrupts the brain's information processing, a number of maladaptive connections may be made instead:

That you are stupid and can't do math

You don't know anything and will fail all math tests

Everyone thinks you are stupid

When groups of people are looking at you they are thinking that you are stupid

It is not OK to make a mistake; making a mistake makes other people angry

You are weak and unable to stand up for yourself when someone is being angry and name-calling

This humiliation has happened once; there is a high risk that it will happen again

Above are two different sets of conclusions and adaptations for the same incident. If the brain has processed the memory properly, then when the same or a similar situation (being called names by an angry person) occurs again, your brain will recall the outcome and decide whether evasive action (such as challenging the person) is needed to avoid that same outcome (feeling humiliated). All of this, by the way, would take place without you ever knowing it. You would feel in control and strong; and any angry, name-callers would have no power over you.

However, if the brain did not fully process the memory at the time, you may feel panic or anger every time you find yourself around short-tempered people and people that remind you of the teacher. You may believe you are unable to stand up for yourself. You may have developed a fear of public speaking because you think all the people that are looking at you think you are stupid. When shopping in stores, you may not trust your math ability and instead rely on assistants to give you the correct change. You may have a dead-end job because you believe you are stupid, and because you failed that math test.

So why are some memories processed and others are not? Why are some people so affected by situations and events, while others are completely unfazed by them? It can depend on the perception of disturbance of the event and the length of time one is exposed to it. Genetics can play a part, as can childhood experiences (someone that has experienced rejection, disappointment, bullying, abuse, humiliation, or parental discord in their early years are more susceptible to Post Traumatic Stress Disorder and other mental health issues.) Fortunately, the brain's ability to process memories adaptively can improve when the 'stuck' memories are finally processed.

THE SYMPTOMS OF TRAUMA

If you are experiencing any of the following symptoms you may be suffering from trauma:

Physical

Extreme alertness - easily startled, hyper-vigilance, hyper-arousal, edginess, jumpiness, agitation, restlessness, feeling 'on guard' or on 'red alert'.

Sleep problems - sleep disturbances, nightmares and bad dreams, insomnia.

Eating problems - eating more or less than normal, a loss of appetite, overeating, comfort eating.

Loss of energy - fatigue, tiredness, exhaustion.

Physical sensations - aches and pains, unexplained pain (especially chest and stomach pain and headaches), chronic pain, muscle tension, nausea, sweating, racing heart, trembling, dizziness.

Sexual dysfunction - loss of libido.

Cognitive

Amnesia - memory lapses, difficulty in recalling information or past events (especially events leading up to, during and after the traumatic event.)

Disturbing, intrusive, repetitive and uncontrollable flashbacks, thoughts, visions, sensations and emotions.

Difficulty concentrating, feelings of being distracted.

Difficulty in decision-making.

Confusion and disorientation, an altered sense of time.

Psychological/ Emotional

Anger, hostility, irritability, resentment, mood swings, emotional reactivity, frequent arguing with loved ones, unprovoked aggression.

Anxiety and fear - general and chronic anxiety, worry, panic attacks, difficulty relaxing.

Depression, despair, sadness, loss of hope, feeling permanently damaged or defective, feeling ineffective, spontaneous crying.

Grief

Guilt, including survivor's guilt, shame, self-blame.

Emotional numbness, shock, disbelief, denial, dissociation, detachment.

11

Sexual problems.

Feeling out of control.

Re-experiencing the traumatic events.

Feelings of being under threat, betrayed and lacking trust in others and oneself, which leads to a sense of detachment and loneliness.

Behaviors

Obsessive and compulsive behavior patterns, including an obsession with death

Impulsive behaviors

Symptoms of ADHD (hyperactivity, inattention, and impulsiveness).

Addictions - Substance abuse, alcoholism, gambling, sex, food, exercise, etc.

Self-harm.

Inability to develop and maintain healthy relationships.

Making self-destructive lifestyle choices.

Avoidance of people, places and activities that are both related and unrelated to a traumatic event

Detachment from other people and emotions, social withdrawal and isolation.

Anhedonia (a loss of interest in hobbies and activities which are normally enjoyable), withdrawal from normal daily routine, loss of previously held beliefs.

Phobias, such as agoraphobia, which can develop as a result of avoidance.

WHY SOME PEOPLE ARE MORE VULNERABLE TO TRAUMA

It's not always the case that a traumatic event (one which most people would assume would be traumatizing) will automatically lead to trauma. Some of us are able to rebound from highly intense and tragic events relatively quickly and without experiencing any long-term issues. Equally, seemingly minor events, which we'd assume would be less upsetting, can sometimes have the most devastating impact on our psychological and emotional health.

If we judge a traumatic event to be small, we may dismiss our feelings, judge our behavior, and come to the conclusion that we are over-reacting. If we decide we are not reacting 'normally' to a major traumatic event we may question whether there is something wrong with us, or worry about an impending nervous breakdown. All of this can increase our feelings of shame and guilt. We need to move away from judging the event and instead focus on understanding the effect it has on us, or the person that is experiencing it.

So are some of us simply more resilient to trauma? And are some of us more vulnerable, or even predisposed, to developing trauma? A number of studies have sought to answer this and have discovered there are factors that may increase our chances of developing trauma and PTSD.

Our current stress level at the time of a traumatic event occurring can have a significant impact. We've probably all experienced periods of stress when we've ended up blowing up over something unimportant. If we are already under a high level of mental stress when an event happens, then our ability to cope may be significantly reduced.

Researchers also found that people with pre-existing trauma are more vulnerable to further (secondary) trauma. Unresolved trauma can have a cumulative effect causing the mind to overload. When there is a backlog, the mind's natural ability to process trauma becomes less effective. Moreover, the mind is more likely to interpret a harmless event as traumatic, thus adding to the unresolved trauma.

Unresolved childhood trauma can also set the stage for secondary trauma. Adults that have been subjected to trauma in their early years may find they are less equipped to deal with life's knocks. For these people, small events can trigger major trauma symptoms.

These research findings explain how an 'insignificant' event, such as receiving a disapproving look, can trigger intense trauma symptoms.

One of the fascinating features of EMDR is that clients don't need to go into detail about the cause of their trauma; they only need to be thinking about it during the therapy. This focus on the trauma rather than the event may be one of the reasons it is effective. It certainly makes it a more user-friendly treatment amongst clients who may be experiencing shame around their symptoms.

THE 3-PRONGED APPROACH

EMDR focuses on 3 areas; past, present and future.

Past Events

Past events, particularly from childhood, can form the foundation of the negative cognitions we hold about ourselves, other people and the world.

If your first experience of a dog was being bitten by it, you may now have a firmly established belief (supported by negative sensations and emotions) that all dogs are dangerous.

Once a belief has formed, the subconscious mind will continue to look for evidence to support it, so you may notice media stories about dogs attacking people, or focus on the barking and snarling of a neighbor's dog as proof they are vicious.

The more supporting evidence the mind finds over time the more deeply ingrained these beliefs become. If a strong association is created between an event and intense negative feelings and sensations, we may start to avoid that event or become 'triggered' when we encounter it in the present moment.

Present Triggers

Usually the reason we seek help for trauma is because our symptoms are affecting us in our daily life. When the same or a similar situation (to the original trauma) occurs, symptoms such as flashbacks, anger, anxiety or depression may be triggered. We may actively avoid situations that we know will trigger our past trauma, as well as hide it from others, which often makes symptoms worse.

Our triggers can extend beyond the original trauma. For example, a person who experienced a car accident may initially avoid driving, but this could progress to avoiding all cars, or developing a fear of all roads even as a pedestrian.

However, sometimes we might not make the connection between our present symptoms and past trauma. This is where EMDR can be used to explore the source of our issues.

Future Events

If an unresolved trauma is affecting you in the present, there is a good chance it will affect you in the future whenever you encounter a similar situation. In some cases, this fear of a re-occurrence of the trauma and the symptoms is entirely rational, particularly if you have a long history of the symptoms being triggered. Other times, you may have overcome most of the initial trauma but feel you lack the skills and confidence to deal with the situation in a different way if you were to face it again. EMDR helps to turn around those beliefs and any lingering worries about future events.

YOUR THERAPY ROOM

It is important to find a quiet room where you won't be disturbed. Ideally, this shouldn't be the place you sleep. You may prefer to sit in a chair or on cushions. Or dim the lights, use candles or work in normal light. Do what you need to do to feel as relaxed and as safe as possible.

Playing relaxing background music is an option. Some people find it distracting while others find it relaxes them and they can notice their thoughts and responses more clearly during the therapy. If you haven't got your own music then YouTube has everything from traditional Chinese music to natural sounds. Pick something long enough to last throughout your session so that you don't have to interrupt your therapy to keep pressing replay.

Most importantly, this therapy space should not have any interruptions or distractions. So switch off your phone and let everyone in the house know you are not to be disturbed.

HOW MANY SESSIONS, HOW OFTEN, AND FOR HOW LONG?

Most therapists recommend around six sessions of EMDR, although for severe trauma a client may need around fifteen sessions, and those with multiple traumas may need many more. Single traumas that have occurred in a healthy adult could be resolved in as few as three sessions. Traumas sustained during childhood will probably require more treatment than if the trauma occurred in adulthood. There is no rule; everyone is different; healing takes as long as it takes.

Typically, most clients have EMDR therapy once a week or every fortnight. The frequency of sessions may be partly down to the cost to the client, but because adaptations continue to take place after EMDR, an adequate break between sessions is needed to allow the mind time to reprocess and recover. However, a recent study into EMDR used the therapy three times a week on its subjects. It found that this concentrated EMDR worked well with no negative or reduced therapeutic effects on the subjects.

To conclude, the amount, frequency, and length of self-administered EMDR sessions, should be down to the individual. You will know when you've reprocessed a trauma and it's time to end the session. You will know when you are recovered from a previous session and are ready for the next. You will know when you have resolved your particular issues and your EMDR treatment is complete.

SIDE EFFECTS

During EMDR therapy, your brain is working hard, making new neurological connections, spring-cleaning the memory and creating new positive beliefs. It can be incredibly draining having to revisit the past that we have avoided for so long.

Other common reactions during and following an EMDR session include headaches, light-headedness, a spaced-out feeling, dizziness, tiredness, and exhaustion. Some clients have reported that their symptoms of anxiety, anger or depression worsen for two or three days following a session while the mind readjusts to the new ways of thinking. If your symptoms are severe to begin with, you should seek professional guidance first.

Because clients are focusing on stressful events, anyone with a heart condition, eye problems, or pregnant women should consult with their doctor or therapist before starting EMDR Therapy.

There have been cases of clients becoming destabilized after EMDR due to undiagnosed dissociative disorders. Good therapists should screen for dissociative disorders before treatment begins and, if present, take more time to work on grounding skills (the preparation stage may take up to six weeks.) Practitioners should take a *fractionation* approach where small elements of a single trauma are worked on at a time to avoid 'flooding' the client.

SELF-ADMINISTERED EMDR THERAPY

The following sections will describe each of the eight-stages that form the framework for EMDR therapy. If you plan to administer the therapy yourself, it is important to follow the procedure just as you would if you were having professional therapy.

THE EIGHT STAGES OF EMDR

1. Personal history and treatment planning
2. Preparation
3. Assessment
4. Desensitization and reprocessing
5. Positive Cognition Installation
6. Body scan
7. Closure
8. Re-evaluation

1. PERSONAL HISTORY & TREATMENT PLANNING

The Planning stage of the EMDR process is largely history taking. The primary aim is to establish the possible targets for treatment.

In a professional setting a therapist will ask a number of questions about your past, present and future. Typically you will be asked why you are seeking help (the Presenting Issue), what your symptoms and behaviors are, and when and where these tend to occur.

With EMDR, you do not need to give specific details about a problem - it can be enough to describe the problem as 'anxiety when public speaking' or 'something that happened at college'.

The associated core beliefs such as *I am helpless* or *I am worthless* can be identified during this stage. A therapist will try to discover the Touchstone Event - or the first occurrence of the problem, and ask you if you can remember any other times when you have felt similar feelings. For clients presenting with multiple issues it can be helpful to group these together.

During this stage it can be beneficial to explore your mother and father's parenting styles, and any significant events that happened during childhood. Whatever comes up for you, no matter how small, it is usually significant. Nobody's childhood is perfect, so if a client is painting a completely happy picture this may be a sign for the therapist to delve deeper. It is rare for a person to lose all of their memories, but gaslighting (where the target's perception of reality is subtly altered to the point they perceive unhealthy behavior as normal,) can be one explanation.

Future triggers, (where you expect an event to reoccur or that you'll feel the same feelings again,) need to be explored. You should identify the skills you need to develop in order to cope with future events. This may be anything from an ability to remain calm to adequate problem solving skills. It is helpful to identify any strengths, positive attitudes and behaviors that you already possess. These can be strengthened during the reprocessing stage of the therapy and used to build your confidence when you are preparing for future events.

As new issues arise during the active therapy sessions, it may be necessary to revisit this planning stage.

If you haven't had professional EMDR before, and this is the first time you've done it yourself, you might want to begin with a minor target event, and then progress onto dealing with the bigger issue(s). This will give you a chance to practice the steps of the procedure and learn to manage any after effects such as tiredness.

2. PREPARATION

During the preparation stage, an EMDR therapist will explain what EMDR is, how it works, and its possible side effects.

While this book provides a foundation of EMDR, Francine Shapiro's book Getting Past Your Past: Take Control of Your Life with Self-Help Techniques from EMDR Therapy goes into detail about the brain science, the preparation techniques and the treatment process, and is recommended further reading for those embarking on solo or practitioner-led EMDR therapy. There are plenty of articles freely available on the internet too.

If you are doing EMDR at home then you are both client and therapist. To understand better what happens during an EMDR session and how to structure it, you may find it useful to watch demonstration videos of sessions on YouTube.

A therapist will spend part of the preparation stage helping you to understand not only the benefits of EMDR, but also the possible side effects. Although everyone is different, EMDR can elicit strong emotions and you should be prepared for this. Side effects can include light-headedness, flashbacks, intrusive thoughts, tiredness or feeling exhausted, headaches, strange dreams, lack of concentration, hyper vigilance and hyper sensitivity, increased emotions and emotional intensity. This is by no means an exhaustive list, nor will everyone who has EMDR experience side effects.

Since the active sessions of EMDR therapy can be intense at times, the therapist must prepare the client by teaching him or her 'grounding techniques' to manage stress. These techniques create a passport back to the present moment, the ability to quickly relax and feel safe again, and to remind you that you're *revisiting* not *reliving* the traumatic experience. Self-soothing tools such as The Butterfly Hug, breathing techniques, Emotional Freedom Technique (tapping), mindfulness, and The Safe Place can be used in between rounds of eye movement processing, as well as in between therapy sessions to manage triggers. These techniques can be easily self-taught and practiced. Empowering yourself with the ability to self-soothe will help you to feel in control during sessions and it is a useful skill for the future in times of stress. Those who are able to manage their own emotions are less susceptible to trauma.

There may be occasions when an EMDR session cannot reach closure. In other words, you've been unable to fully process and reprogram a target memory during one session. There are a number of reasons for this. It could simply be because the session time has come to an end or you are tired and choose to finish early. Sometimes a target memory has more layers to it than first thought and it is only during the session that you, or your therapist, realize more than one session is required to tackle it. You can pick up where you left off the next time, but in these cases the grounding tools are important to manage any flashbacks, feelings and thoughts and that may come up in the meantime.

GROUNDING EXERCISES

To remain grounded during sessions, and to enable you to cope with your emotions during the weeks and months of treatment, a therapist will teach you a variety of emotional stability and relaxation techniques. Breathing techniques, meditation, mindfulness, self-hypnosis, physical exercise etc, can help you manage your symptoms, but two techniques that benefit EMDR clients in particular are The Safe Place and The Butterfly Hug.

The Safe Place

Take slow breaths and focus on a safe and calm place in your mind. It could be real or imagined. Use all of your senses and focus on the sights, sounds and smells of your safe place. This can be difficult to begin with, but with daily five-minute practice you will be able to transport yourself to your safe place whenever you need to. Having a photograph of the place in front of you can make this exercise a lot easier.

The Butterfly Hug

The butterfly hug has been used to calm and soothe people caught up in natural disasters and other traumatic events. It is effective in times of great emotional distress. Cross your arms and rest each hand on the opposite shoulder. Focus on your breathing, and maybe bring to mind the image of your safe place. When you begin to feel calmer you can tap your hands alternately on each shoulder six times. Take a breath and repeat if necessary.

3. ASSESSMENT

The assessment stage has three parts to it.

1. Form a picture of the target event
2. Identify the associated negative belief
3. Identify an alternative positive belief

1. Form a Picture of the Target Event

If the target event causes an emotional reaction in you then it will probably be easy to form a 'picture' of the incident. Perhaps a person, a place, or an activity causes an immediate physiological reaction in you, triggering certain thoughts and feelings. Often this image is something we avoid thinking about because it brings about unpleasant sensations. It is important to remember that thoughts are just thoughts, but if you find yourself becoming ungrounded and reliving the image then you probably need to break the picture down into more manageable images, perhaps even focusing on smell or sound first.

Once you have it formed a picture your mind, scale it using the 0-10 units of disturbance scale (with 0 being no effect and 10 being extremely disturbing.) Take written notes of the body sensations you feel when you think about the event, and note where in your body you experience them.

Some events may not have a visual image associated with them (perhaps because they occurred very early in childhood.) EMDR can still work effectively on implicit memories. For these traumas, the sensations or feelings are your 'picture' and this is what you should focus on during treatment. A visual image of the event may come up for you during the session and provide you with better insight into the issue you have.

2. Identify the Associated Negative Belief

Every experience we have helps to shape our beliefs. Each of the traumatic experiences you listed in your personal history will have taught you something negative about yourself or the world, even if you have not been consciously aware of it.

Francine Shapiro's Book Getting Past Your Past identified three categories of negative beliefs:

1. Responsibility (feeling defective in some way, such as unlovable, ugly, or not good enough.)

2. Lack of safety (such as feeling in danger)

3. Lack of control (such as feeling overpowered, unable to stand up for oneself, or feeling that no one can be trusted.)

During this assessment stage you'll need to identify the belief(s) you learned from the target incidents. Your present-day behavior and emotions may give you a clue as to what beliefs you have taken from a past experience. Sometimes though, you may not yet be able to identify a negative belief. This is OK. The negative beliefs you have been carrying will usually show themselves during reprocessing.

3. Identifying an Alternative Positive Belief

EMDR not only desensitizes traumas, but it enables clients to replace the negative beliefs they learned with a positive cognition. So *I am a disappointment* is changed to *I am Ok the way I am*, and *I am not safe*, is changed to *I am safe now. I am unlovable/ ugly/ weak/ inadequate/ bad /stupid/ anxious*, are changed to *I am lovable /beautiful /strong/ worthwhile/ good/ smart/ calm*.

When you have decided what new belief you would like to install, think about how much you believe it, this time on a scale of 0-7 (with 0 being not at all, and 7 being that you completely believe it.) Note down the number.

NEGATIVE & POSITIVE COGNITIONS

You can use the list below to identify the negative beliefs you have. Think about the target event and read through the list to see if any phrases seem true to you.

You could also read through the list without thinking of any specific moments in your life. If there are any positive beliefs you don't believe about yourself you can explore the issues around them using EMDR.

Negative/Positive Cognitions List of Examples

I am a bad person / I am a good loving person
I am unlovable / I am lovable
I am terrible / I am fine as I am
I am inadequate / I am OK as I am
I am worthless / I am worthy, I am worthwhile
I am shameful / I am honorable
I am not good enough / I am good enough, I am enough
I am permanently damaged / I am healthy, I can be healthy
I am ugly / I am attractive, lovable
I am stupid / I am smart, intelligent
I am insignificant / I am significant, I am important
I am unimportant / I am important
I am a disappointment / I am okay the way I am
I am different / I am OK as I am
I do not belong/ I am OK as I am
I deserve to be miserable / I deserve to be happy
I deserve to die / I deserve to live
I do not deserve___ / I can have___, I am deserving
I only deserve bad things / I deserve good things
I don't deserve love / I deserve love; I can have love
I am in danger / It is over, I am safe now
I am not safe / I am safe
I cannot relax / I can relax and be myself
I am not in control / I am now in control
I am helpless / I now have choices
I am powerless / I now have choices

I cannot cope / I can handle it
I am weak / I am strong
I cannot trust anyone / I can choose who to trust
I cannot be trusted / I can trust myself
I cannot trust myself / I can learn to trust myself
I cannot trust my judgment / I can trust my judgment
I cannot let it out / I can choose to let it out
I cannot show my emotions / I can choose to show my emotions
I cannot protect myself / I can (learn) to protect myself
I should have done something / I did the best I could in that situation
I did something wrong / I learned (can learn) from it
I cannot get what I need / I can get what I need
I cannot get what I want / I can get what I want
I am a failure / I can succeed
I cannot succeed / I can succeed
I have to be perfect / I can be myself
I can't make mistakes / I am free to be myself

4. DESENSITIZATION AND REPROCESSING

The desensitization and reprocessing stage is where active therapy takes place. It is when the mind finally completes its processing of the target event.

You will begin by recalling the picture of the target memory as defined in the assessment stage. Allow yourself to feel the negative emotions and sensations associated with it. This should not feel like an overwhelming or frightening experience; you are revisiting the event not reliving it. If you struggle to stay grounded while doing this, then you should seek guidance from a professional who can teach you how in just one or two sessions.

Once you are focused on the target event, and are feeling its associated sensations, then bilateral stimulation can begin. Bilateral stimulation involves moving your eyes from side to side, following a therapist's hand (or a light on a screen) while keeping your head still. If you are doing this at home without a therapist, you can search YouTube for self-administered EMDR videos. Some EMDR videos are silent while others use isochronic sounds for added therapeutic effect. Experiment in the first few sessions of your self-guided therapy to find one that works best for you.

During the bilateral stimulation you will not enter a trance, be hypnotized, or experience an altered state of awareness. You will be fully conscious throughout and always in control of your own mind and the therapy session.

Each set of the bilateral stimulation can last between 30 seconds to 3 minutes. Just notice whatever comes to mind, and let whatever happens, happen. After each round of bilateral stimulation, take a deep breath, and notice whatever comes to your mind. It may help to jot down notes of the thoughts, images, beliefs, words, and sensations that arise during and between each set, just as a therapist would. These insights can guide the session and also help you to make sense of the trauma.

Try not to judge what should come up. Sometimes we can go into an EMDR session with rigid ideas of the causes of a trauma. But EMDR can lead you to surprising insights and connections. Like the pieces of a jigsaw suddenly fitting together, you realize life events are linked and everything makes a lot more sense.

Each time something new pops up in your mind, focus on it and then use bilateral stimulation again. Repeat this process until nothing else comes up for you. When you think of the target memory, along with all of its details, it should be zero on the 0-10 scale of disturbance.

It should be noted that this stage of the therapy can be an emotional roller coaster. You are opening old wounds and revisiting painful memories, albeit from a place of safety. You may feel a range of emotions such as sadness, rage, hurt, and anxiety, before the mind lets it go and then you will feel calm, relief, happy, and lighter. As mentioned above, you should try to let emotions flow as they arise, rather than judge what you should be feeling. If you're processing a betrayal in a relationship for instance, you would probably expect to feel anger. However, you may process the anger early on and then find sadness and feelings of unworthiness were lurking underneath, and beneath that, a memory of a parent's betrayal that also needs to be reprocessed. Sometimes we like to cling on to certain emotions because they mask the deeper more painful issues. This is what we mean when we talk about the many layers of trauma that EMDR can uncover.

5. POSITIVE COGNITION INSTALLATION

When the target event has been neutralized (i.e. it has become a zero on the emotional disturbance scale), then it is time to replace the negative cognition with a positive cognition. Before the reprocessing began, you should have selected a new positive belief such as *I am worthy*, *I am safe*, or *I now have choices*.

It is possible that the negative belief you identified in the assessment stage was not the problem after all. If you need to change the positive cognition you want to install then do so. You can also install multiple positive cognitions if you need to and have time.

On a scale of 0-7 (with 0 being not at all and 7 being completely) how much do you believe the positive statement in relation to the original target event? Focus on the new picture, feelings, words and sensations of this new belief, and begin the bilateral stimulation again, in the same way you did when you were working on the old painful memory. Each time you complete a set, notice how you feel, and ask yourself how much you believe the new cognition on the scale of 0-7. Apply the bilateral stimulation until it becomes a 7. To reinforce the new cognition, use a final 30-second burst of eye movements.

At this stage you will be in a receptive frame of mind and this may be a good time to reinforce any other positive cognitions you have installed in previous EMDR work. However, do not force these additional positive cognitions. It is better to end a session on a positive note, rather than being frustrated because you've tried to force another. This latter stage of the therapy is probably the time when you will feel the most tired and your concentration may start to diminish, therefore, as long as one positive belief has been installed, you can always work on others during your next session.

6. BODY SCAN

The body scan is the final check to ensure the target event has been fully desensitized, reprocessed and reprogrammed.

To perform the body scan, breathe slowly and get into a relaxed, grounded state. Then think of the original target event. Run through it slowly, as though you are watching a movie, and scan your body from head to toe. At this stage of EMDR therapy, clients are often tired and relaxed so noticing tension in the body is much easier. If any negative emotions, tension or other physical sensations occur while you are doing this, apply short 30-second bursts of bilateral stimulation, and then scan your body again.

Do the same for the new positive belief and look for areas of tension where you might be holding back from fully accepting the new cognition. When you can think about the target event without experiencing tension in the body, processing is complete. If you can think about the target event and feel good about yourself, then the new positive belief has taken effect.

7. CLOSURE

The end of every EMDR session should bring a sense of closure. This is chiefly a time when you get to relax after all the work you've done.

A professional therapist should never allow a client to leave their office feeling worse than when they came in, and this is a good moment to summarize what you have achieved and acknowledge your effort. Clients in professional therapy are reminded of what to expect until their next session (possible flashbacks etc), and encouraged to keep a log of thoughts, emotions and behavior changes. Clients should be reminded to take care of themselves and allow plenty of recovery time before the next session. After intense EMDR, it is recommended that you don't drive.

Some target events may require more than one session to be fully resolved. In these cases the therapist must make sure you have the tools to cope until the next session. The Butterfly Technique, self-care, breathing, and other techniques learned during the preparation stage can help reduce any emotional symptoms you may experience until your next EMDR therapy session. You can also give yourself a boost by reminding yourself how much of the target memory you have already worked through.

In self-guided EMDR, you can give yourself extra time to come to a resolution in the one session, or if you are getting tired, at least try to end your session with a positive cognition, such as *I can work to resolve this*, or *I can overcome this*. Use bilateral stimulation until you believe the statement, and even if the target event hasn't been entirely reprocessed yet you will still feel optimistic.

With a thorough history treatment plan though, this situation can often be avoided. Major traumatic events should be broken down into more manageable target events and treated over several sessions.

8. RE-EVALUATION

Professional EMDR practitioners should always start a session by asking their client what changes they have noticed since their last session. Keeping a record of things that happen (good or bad) in between therapy sessions will help you see the changes EMDR is having. It can be a source of much-needed motivation as well as a guide to what still needs to be worked on.

For example, you may notice yourself handling a situation in a better way, and that your trigger doesn't feel as intense, but some other negative thoughts and images came up relating to another (new target) event. EMDR peels away the layers of memories; once you have reprocessed one memory, you may well find another one lurking underneath that needs reprocessing too. You may also find that you remember extra details about the target event. This may just require a few short bursts of bilateral stimulation to desensitize it at the start of the session and then to reinforce the positive cognition.

Once the re-evaluation has been dealt with, you can move on to dealing with the next target event or aspect of the trauma.

REFERENCES & RESOURCES

References
Grimley, B. The Psychologist, (August 2014). EMDR – origins and anomalies, 27(8), Letters.

Shapiro, F. (1989). Efficacy of the eye movement desensitization procedure in the treatment of traumatic memories. Journal of Traumatic Stress, 2, 199–223.

Shapiro, F. (2001). Eye movement desensitization and reprocessing: Basic principles, protocols and procedures (2nd ed.). New York: Guilford Press.

Shapiro, F. (2012). Getting Past Your Past: Take Control of Your Life with Self-Help Techniques from EMDR Therapy.

Resources
Bilateral Stimulation Videos
http://www.youtube.com/watch?v=eZkdh5dVksw
http://www.youtube.com/watch?v=OlfQIRJEsYk
https://www.youtube.com/watch?v=DALbwI7m1vM

EMDR Session Demonstration Videos
http://www.youtube.com/watch?v=KpRQvcW2kUM
https://www.youtube.com/watch?v=L6UvKhLYf7w

EMDR Theory Video
http://www.youtube.com/watch?v=9o0JaecxPkY

Books
Getting Past Your Past: Take Control of Your Life with Self-Help Techniques from EMDR Therapy. Francine Shapiro, Rodale Books, 2013

Websites
www.emdr.com
emdria.site-ym.com

WORKBOOK

EMDR SESSION PROMPT SHEET

Once the history and preparation stages are complete this is how EMDR therapy should proceed:

ASSESSMENT

Form a picture of the target event
Note body sensations and scale level of disturbance 0-10
Identify the associated negative belief
Identify an alternative positive belief, scale it 0-7

DESENSITIZATION AND REPROCESSING

Recall the picture of the target memory
Use sets of bilateral stimulation for 30 seconds to 3 minutes
Notice whatever comes to mind; let whatever happens, happen
Repeat bilateral stimulation until nothing else comes up

POSITIVE COGNITION INSTALLATION

Focus on the image, words, and feelings of the new positive belief
Use sets of bilateral stimulation until it becomes a '7' on the 0-7 scale
Use a final 30-second burst to reinforce the new cognition
Work on other negative thoughts if you want to

BODY SCAN

Recall the original target event
If tension is present use short bursts of bilateral stimulation

CLOSURE

Always try to end a session on a positive note
Relax and focus on your achievements
If target event is not resolved install a positive cognition: 'I can resolve this.'
Use relaxation and emotion stabilizing techniques until the next session

RE-EVALUATION

Note your thoughts and feelings in between sessions
Begin your next session by working on residual negative thoughts with bilateral stimulation

Your History

As you fill in your history, don't think about the details; simply write down keywords and bullet points. Then, put a star next to your ten most distressing events and issues.

PAST

Write a list of memories and past events that cause you anguish.

PRESENT

Write a list of your current issues and triggers. Note the thoughts, feelings and sensations that usually come up in these challenging situations.

FUTURE

Write a list of future situations that are likely to trigger your symptoms. Are there any situations or people you will avoid because of your symptoms? What skills or qualities do you feel you lack? What are your personal goals?

You may want to use colors or symbols to highlight patterns and links between your past, present and future.

Grounding Exercise Daily Log

Practice grounding techniques (The Safe Place, The Butterfly Hug, or other techniques such as mindfulness, meditation, or breathing exercises,) to prepare for the active therapy sessions.

DAY	EXERCISE	NOTES
1		
2		
3		
4		
5		
6		
7		
8		
9		
10		
11		
12		
13		
14		
15		
16		
17		
18		
19		
20		
21		
22		
23		
24		
25		
26		
27		
28		

Target event_____

Assessment

Form a picture of the target event

Identify the associated negative belief

Identify an alternative positive belief(s)

Desensitization

Notes from bilateral stimulation

(lined note space)

Disturbance Scale: Neutral **0 1 2 3 4 5 6 7 8 9 10** Disturbing

45

Reprocessing
New Positive Belief(s)

Closure

In this session I have achieved

I look forward to

Re-evaluation

During the week I experienced the following (thoughts, emotions, behavior changes, dreams etc)

Things I still need to work on are

Target event_____

Assessment

Form a picture of the target event

Identify the associated negative belief

Identify an alternative positive belief(s)

Desensitization
Notes from bilateral stimulation

Reprocessing

New Positive Belief(s)

Closure

In this session I have achieved

I look forward to

53

Re-evaluation

During the week I experienced the following (thoughts, emotions, behavior changes, dreams etc)

Things I still need to work on are

Target event_____

Assessment

Form a picture of the target event

Identify the associated negative belief

Identify an alternative positive belief(s)

Desensitization

Notes from bilateral stimulation

Reprocessing

New Positive Belief(s)

Disbelieve **0 1 2 3 4 5 6 7** Believe

Closure

In this session I have achieved

I look forward to

Re-evaluation

During the week I experienced the following (thoughts, emotions, behavior changes, dreams etc)

Things I still need to work on are

Target event_____

Assessment

Form a picture of the target event

_____

Identify the associated negative belief

Identify an alternative positive belief(s)

Desensitization

Notes from bilateral stimulation

Disturbance Scale: Neutral **0 1 2 3 4 5 6 7 8 9 10** Disturbing

63

Reprocessing

New Positive Belief(s)

Closure

In this session I have achieved

I look forward to

Re-evaluation

During the week I experienced the following (thoughts, emotions, behavior changes, dreams etc)

Things I still need to work on are

Target event_____

Assessment

Form a picture of the target event

_____
_____
_____
_____
_____
_____
_____
_____
_____
_____
_____
_____
_____
_____
_____
_____
_____
_____
_____
_____
_____
_____
_____
_____
_____
_____
_____
_____
_____

Disturbance Scale: Neutral **0 1 2 3 4 5 6 7 8 9 10** Disturbing

Identify the associated negative belief

Identify an alternative positive belief(s)

Desensitization

Notes from bilateral stimulation

Reprocessing

New Positive Belief(s)

Disbelieve **0 1 2 3 4 5 6 7** Believe

Closure

In this session I have achieved

I look forward to

Re-evaluation

During the week I experienced the following (thoughts, emotions, behavior changes, dreams etc)

Things I still need to work on are

Target event_____

Assessment

Form a picture of the target event

Identify the associated negative belief

Identify an alternative positive belief(s)

Desensitization

Notes from bilateral stimulation

Reprocessing

New Positive Belief(s)

Disbelieve **0 1 2 3 4 5 6 7** Believe

Closure

In this session I have achieved

I look forward to

Re-evaluation

During the week I experienced the following (thoughts, emotions, behavior changes, dreams etc)

Things I still need to work on are

Target event_____

Assessment
Form a picture of the target event

Identify the associated negative belief

Identify an alternative positive belief(s)

Desensitization
Notes from bilateral stimulation

Reprocessing
New Positive Belief(s)

Disbelieve **0 1 2 3 4 5 6 7** Believe

Closure

In this session I have achieved

I look forward to

Re-evaluation

During the week I experienced the following (thoughts, emotions, behavior changes, dreams etc)

Things I still need to work on are

Target event_____

Assessment

Form a picture of the target event

Disturbance Scale: Neutral **0 1 2 3 4 5 6 7 8 9 10** Disturbing

Identify the associated negative belief

Identify an alternative positive belief(s)

Desensitization

Notes from bilateral stimulation

Reprocessing

New Positive Belief(s)

Disbelieve **0 1 2 3 4 5 6 7** Believe

Closure

In this session I have achieved

I look forward to

Re-evaluation

During the week I experienced the following (thoughts, emotions, behavior changes, dreams etc)

Things I still need to work on are

Target event_____

Assessment

Form a picture of the target event

Identify the associated negative belief

Identify an alternative positive belief(s)

Desensitization
Notes from bilateral stimulation

Reprocessing

New Positive Belief(s)

Closure

In this session I have achieved

I look forward to

Re-evaluation

During the week I experienced the following (thoughts, emotions, behavior changes, dreams etc)

Things I still need to work on are

Target event_____

Assessment

Form a picture of the target event

Identify the associated negative belief

Identify an alternative positive belief(s)

Desensitization
Notes from bilateral stimulation

Reprocessing

New Positive Belief(s)

Disbelieve **0 1 2 3 4 5 6 7** Believe

100

Closure

In this session I have achieved

I look forward to

Re-evaluation

During the week I experienced the following (thoughts, emotions, behavior changes, dreams etc)

Things I still need to work on are

JOURNAL

Made in the USA
Las Vegas, NV
06 August 2023

75723999R00090